Scottish Castles

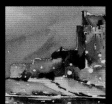

Published by Jonathan Wheeler Art

www.jonathanwheelerart.com

email: jonathan@soulofscotland.co.uk

telephone: +44(0) 1309 692202

Copyright © 2012 Jonathan Wheeler Art

All rights reserved. No part of this publication may be reproduced, stored in a retrieval system, or transmitted in any form or by any means, electronic, mechanical, photocopying, recording or otherwise without the prior permission of the copyright owner.

Thanks to Kevin Wheeler, Marilza Padialli, Kate Williams MacKenzie, Jenny Baker, Liz Huddleston, Karin Thain, Pete Martin and Andy Macdonald

ISBN 978-0-9572792-0-9

Printed in Scotland by Allander Print Ltd

WORLD LAND TRUST™

www.carbonbalancedpaper.com
CBP0004782805125432

MIX
Paper from responsible sources
FSC® C008886

Contents | pages

Soul of Scotland

What draws you to a castle? A castle emanates history, power, mystery and legend. Hewn from rock: majestic, mighty and bold — those walls have witnessed every action mankind could make and every emotion a person could feel. Hundreds of years have steeped them in desire and hatred, bravery and cowardice, joy and despair — the myriad of colours that make up our lives. They have seen injustice, the battles of the few against the many, the birth and death of kings and queens, and they have listened to intrigue and plots for revenge. They may be slumbering now, but our castles know what they have seen. It is written in their walls.

Passions are important, and maybe your enthusiasm is for timelines, armoury, battle strategy or customs — visit the castles and they will tell you all you need to know. Look beyond though, and you will know that castles have old souls. There is a change in the air that surrounds them. Castles can renew a weary spirit, and without even trying they can take up a place in your heart. Perhaps in a virtual world accessed through cables and wires, castles remind us who we really are, where we have come from, what we are capable of, and where we might go.

In this book we hope to capture a little of the spirit of these beautiful old keepers of the Scottish soul.

Edinburgh Castle

The Lion Rampant

Seagulls wheel over granite rocks. Towering ramparts rise up from sheer cliff faces and blackened cannon point out across the roofs. It is a city in the sky, chilled by the winds of war. Cobbled streets glint underfoot and the cold hard steel of weaponry glistens in the sun. Edinburgh Castle is the royal blue and golden ochre of infant kings, it is the soft white ermine and blood-red rubies of would-be queens and it is the proud and rampant lion of the Scottish soul.

Is there an ancient beat of recognition in our hearts when we look up to this fortress on a hill? Is there a deep and primordial sense that this was once the pulsing heart of our world? Look through the corner of your eye. Put away your camera and forget about your packed lunch. Unplug your audio tour. Slip away to find a quiet space. Touch an ancient wall or feel the earth. You stand in the same place as Charles 1 on the eve of becoming King of Scotland; as Mary Queen of Scots, pregnant with the future king; as Queen Margaret when she heard the news of her husband's death.

Is it not amazing that this is the same stone that those kings and queens have touched; the same ground upon which they walked? Three hundred, five hundred, one thousand years of history — this place has witnessed it all.

Whether by stealth or siege, Edinburgh Castle changed its keepers many times. The final outcome each time was usually bloody and brutal. Imagine looking up to the castle overhead and seeing the flames from four beacons against the night sky, signalling that the castle was under attack. Imagine the sound of bugles and drums carried on the thick sea mist that swirled around the castle's base. Imagine the sheer smooth curve of the Half Moon Battery walls with bronze cannon pointing outwards ready to defend. To the assailant, these walls held the threat of death. To those inside, the walls held the promise of protection.

Mighty and iconic, Edinburgh Castle tells Scotland's story.

The Black Dinner 1440

The dark castle tower is prepared for the banquet. The candles flicker on the faces of those gathered there, the Black Douglases — the sixth Earl of Douglas and his brother, invited by Sir William Crichton, Governor of the Castle. The child king, ten years old, sits at the head of the table, animated by the talk amongst his guests. The feast is an offer of reconciliation between the families, an end to their feuds.

The doors burst open and the bloodied head of a bull is placed with a flourish before them. Its significance? A token of condemnation to death. Wrestled roughly to an adjoining room, the guests are subjected to a cursory trial for treason. They are found guilty, and dragged from the room, their young king's pleas for mercy left unheard. He could only watch as they met their brutal fate, in the name of the Crown.

Eilean Donan Castle

From Ashes to Castle of Dreams

A fortress stands proudly where three lochs meet — guarding, watching and waiting — the Keeper of the Sea Kingdom. The backdrop is of pebbled shores and steep-sided misty mountains, opalescent reflections of amethyst, emerald and cerulean blue. Centre stage is the stillness and beauty of a perfect Scottish castle on an island in a loch. The curved arches of the bridge lead out to the towering stone walls — the focus for a world of cameras, but once the focus of a darker eye.

There are shadows on the walls of this castle. Memories are of wilder times, when the sea brought warlords and warriors to the gates, and fearful menace on its waves.

For two centuries the ruins lay alone, silent and abandoned against the stillness of the loch. But one man's vision brought the five-hundred-year seat of the Clan MacRae back to life. Horse-drawn stone, green slate and pine-scented firs were cut, crafted and hewn, and the image of Eilean Donan was reborn. The vision of Farquar MacRae, and the renaissance of an icon.

Death of a Castle — May 10th, 1719

A soldier far from home walked the lonely ramparts and Jacobite men gathered silently in the hills. The word was out, the landing would come, their ranks would be swelled. But the sea carried a malevolent guest. That day the loch was alive, angry waves swelled by the wind and driving rain. Three naval ships cut their way through the churning water, moving in on their quarry, with one hundred guns of war, rows of sails battered by the storm, rows of cannon trained on the castle walls.

Three days of assault began. Screams were carried through the air, walls were pounded and broken in smoke-filled terror. There would be no flags of truce. The might of the English navy bore down on its prey. Only forty men were inside, fighting for their cause. Outnumbered and outgunned, the castle fought to the end. Barrels of gunpowder finished the castle. The final roar signalled the moment of death, tremors coursing through the pine-clad valleys. Only the blackened, broken bones of war remained.

Dunnottar Castle

Mighty Defender of the Sea

Surrounded by the crashing waves of the North Sea, the mighty walls of Dunnottar rise up from cliffs of sheer salt-bitten granite.

Lie down on the cliff top, and look through the tufts of windblown grass to the edge of the ocean. Let many centuries drift away. Lift your eyes to the distant horizon and picture the Viking longships with rows of oars and coloured sails preparing to attack. Imagine the boats laden with weapons of war, and the savage cries that carried across the waves.

Imagine, four centuries ago, the fear inside those mighty walls as Cromwell's army fought to capture the Honours of Scotland held within. Look down the sheer cliff face to the pebbled shore and imagine a tiny figure — a lone woman collecting wood and seaweed for her home. In her arms she hides precious symbols of Scottish nationhood, lowered from the walls; a crown, sceptre and sword. Carried to safety and buried deep in the shelter of a church, the jewels were spared.

The castle fell, but the honour of Scotland remained.

Crathes Castle

Baronial Towers and Turrets

Through bottle-green hedges of Irish yew and avenues of limes, the slender, pink-harled walls of Crathes Castle rise up against the Deeside sky. Smooth, round turrets are topped with slate-grey spirals, corbels and clocks.

Inside, narrow stone stairs twist and turn into warm golden rooms dappled in light, safely cocooned from the outside world. There are painted ceilings of cobalt and ochre, and vaulted carved arches of tawny oak.

Crathes is the ancestral seat of the Burnetts of Leys — generals, admirals, judges and bishops — a castle that surrounded its family with strong protective arms.

But secrets lie behind these walls and under the velvety soft cover of nightfall, stories are told that chill the soul. Tales of a girl and her baby seen crossing the room, and the bones of a woman and child disturbed beneath the floor. Secrets that only the walls of Crathes Castle can know, and answers that no-one living can give.

Fyvie Castle | Five Towers

The five towers of Fyvie stand tall and magnificent against the Aberdeenshire sky. Five Scottish families — Seton, Meldrum, Preston, Gordon and Leith; each a tower to call their own. Shrouded in mystery, curses and folklore, with tales of secret chambers and magical stones, the

castle stands proudly over the swirling river Ythan. Inside, Edwardian grandeur has grown from medieval roots. Walls that saw Alexander II, William the Lion and Robert the Bruce, are now hung with Gainsboroughs and Raeburns in elegant drawing rooms. Outside, the castle clock looks down onto smooth green lawns that lead through oaks and ashes to a shimmering lake. Wrought-iron gates open onto woodland gardens that overflow with Scottish fruit and flowers.

Stirling Castle

Crowns, Sceptres and Swords

The royal castle towers against the skyline, indomitable and mighty. Sheer grey walls rise out of basalt and greenstone, protecting the Great Hall's limewashed splendour.
The rain-drenched slated roofs of Stirling city shimmer in the castle's shadow. Destined to be fought over, contested and besieged, Stirling Castle was the glittering brooch joining north and south, and the lofty symbol of power and control.

A gateway of soaring towers and impregnable walls, seen for miles around, proclaims the entrance to a magnificent royal residence for the Stewart kings. Through the arches, the ancient walls watched over Mary Queen of Scots as she grew, and saw the Chapel Royal decked in pomp and splendour as she was crowned.

From its walls, the broken and bloodied body of the eighth Earl of Douglas was thrown to the ground below, murdered at the hands of James II. It was inside these walls that Robert the Bruce drank to the savage defeat of the English and outside these walls that Bonnie Prince Charlie made a last futile attempt to claim the castle for the Jacobite cause.

Look out from the rugged stone walls to the east. Down below on the fertile plains of Stirling, bloody battles were won and lost, with names that are etched on the country's soul. Stirling Bridge, when the giant sword of William Wallace brought down the might of Edward's army. Bannockburn, two days of death and glory that defined Scotland.

The Battle of Bannockburn — Midsummer 1314

Dawn broke over the field of battle. Banners fluttered, armour glinted and preparations were made. Excitement coursed through the veins, hearts pulsed with fear. The hour had come to fight. A shout went up and hung in the air. The knights on their horses emerged from the ranks. Immense, highly trained, they were the fighting elite. Slowly at first then gaining speed, the thunder of hooves on turf, lances lowered, horses spurred on, visors shut fast, side by side galloping towards their fate, towards the brutal spears held fast by the Scots.

Order became chaos in the blood-red frenzy of battle. The headlong onslaught of sword on dagger, of arrow on shield, of hand on hand.

Liberty in every blow — this was the hour when freedom and pride met dominion and power. This was the day when thousands of sons, brothers, fathers and husbands would die.

Cawdor Castle

Be Mindful

Turrets and towers rise up through lavender and yew, roses sway against ivy-clad walls. Wild verdant woodland beckons through old wooden gates, and an amber burn cascades beneath the windows, filling each room with its sound.

Cross the drawbridge and you are under the spell. There are tales of romance, of kings and thanes, lives of excess and murder most foul. Captivating, enchanting, but dangerous to know. Cawdor is the light and dark of Scottish perfection. You are welcomed in, but left wanting more. Mind your head and mind your heart.

Seven hundred years as a home to the thanes of Cawdor, and the fires are still lit, beds are still slept in. Maybe Cawdor's spell is in the weaving of the old and the new, sparked by the warmth that comes from a living castle.

Let the words of the 6th Earl of Cawdor take you along the tartan passageways and the shadowy vaults of the tower. Let him tell you stories of rich Flemish tapestries, an old twisted holly tree, flint-lock muskets and a glory hole.

Muriel's Story 1498 - 1573

The Campbells of Inverliever came for Muriel of Calder one night. She was barely eighteen months old, but heiress to the Cawdor estates. Wrested from the arms of her nurse, pursued but not saved, the tiny hostage was brought safely to her captor, the Lord of Argyll, on the shores of Loch Awe. At twelve years old, the flame haired girl from Cawdor was married to Sir John Campbell, Argyll's second son. Two powerful clans became one.

An arranged alliance perhaps, in the midst of clan rivalries and in-laws with unsettled scores, but a lifelong and happy marriage for Muriel and John. The union of the Campbells of Cawdor, sealed by the birth of seven children, and a destiny lived out to the present day.

Linlithgow Palace

Grandeur, Power and Royalty

The towers and turrets of a royal palace rise imperiously over a shimmering loch. The crystal water of a fountain cascades over unicorns and lions, and swallows dive between the eaves. Only the bare bones of the bedchambers and banquet halls of kings remain — the ghosts of a pleasure palace.

This was once the magnificent court of the Stewart kings. From the ashes of a fire, James I built his renaissance palace, a sumptuous loch side haven between the castles of Stirling and Edinburgh. In later years, it was a palatial wedding gift from James IV to his wife Margaret Tudor.

Picture the Great Hall hundreds of years ago. Tapestries of rainbow threads cover the walls, huge oak beams arch overhead. The king is sitting under the light of the great window, and whole tree trunks burn in a fireplace that fills a wall. Tables groan under spit-roast beef, lamb and geese, gallons of ale, and sheaves of fresh bread. The hall is alive with music and laughter.

Close your eyes and let the ghosts entertain you.

Castle Fraser

Turrets and Towers

Shafts of early morning sunlight catch the dewdrops sprinkled across the grass. An oak-lined avenue slopes down towards the majestic turrets and towers of a chateau. Gables and balustrades reach proudly towards the sky, amidst the rolling hills of Aberdeenshire.

A golden weathervane perched on the dizzying heights of an ancient baronial tower, glints as it turns. It looks across cattle-studded fields to Bennachie and down to the Don. Inside, there are great halls with portraits, trophies and stags. Look closer still and there are trap doors and secret stairs, and careless whispers overheard. And all the while, drifting like ether through the ancient rooms, there are tales of royal murders that chill the soul.

St Andrews Castle

The Ancient Stage of Mitres and Crowns

The cold blue waters of the North Sea lap calmly against the time-worn rocks. Seagulls swoop and cry across the headland, and on the golden crescent of Castle Sands children net crabs in the shadow of the walls. In the distance, trawlers cut through the waves to the harbours of Crail, St. Monans and Elie.

Once a magnificent coastal stage for the mighty home of the Scottish church — with walls that were vibrant with the purple and royal blue colours of archbishops and kings. A castle that was the ancient seat of the Bishop of Alba, where James the third was born and where James the first was once taught — and a theatre where scenes of suspicion, murder and revenge were played out.

Six hundred years of learning and worship infused in the stone, and centuries of turmoil steeped in the soil.

Urquhart Castle

By Sword and Fire

An ancient ruin, beautiful and defiant, stands unflinching against the inky depths of a glittering loch. Shadows pass over the water, and mystery moves in the moonless depths below. A solitary tower proudly displays its battle scars, a Scottish flag flies alongside. Jagged stones lie where they fell, against the rise and fall of leaf-green banks. Dark shrouded mountains of heather and pine stretch out beneath storm-heavy skies, whilst the sun's rays chase clouds across distant shores.

Urquhart has lived its life by sword and fire. In its once burning embers there are stories of Picts, Jacobites and Lords of the Isles.

The year is 1395. The galleys of the Lords of the Isles emerge from the spectral mist that hangs over the loch, the figure of Donald Macdonald at the helm. The ships slide through ebony waters, towards their prey.

The outline of the castle, mighty and timeworn, stands silhouetted against a twilight sky and the golden flames from its fires are reflected in the ice cold water. The sound of laughter and feasting, careless and blithe, drifts down from towering walls. But tonight there will be a battle. Swords, arrows and axes will come together to decide the fate of the glen.

As a blood-red dawn breaks over the loch, the last weapon falls to the ground and the last cry echoes across the water.

As the shafts of morning sunlight stretch across the valley, the cruel plunder begins. Cattle, horses and sheep are driven from the glen, a mighty haul and rich spoils for the victors. The carcass of a community is left picked clean to the bones — stripped of livelihoods, homes and dignity. Amidst the empty fields and broken walls, the people of Glen Urquhart must start again.

St. Columba and the Pictish Kingdom

Two thousand years of mystery weigh heavy in the air. Look down the vast dark loch from the grey-pebbled shore. Fourteen centuries ago, an Irish prince and priest walked the ominous water's edge, spreading his Christian word to the Picts. Tall, charismatic and strong, St. Columba travelled to the court of King Brude through the wild forests and fields of the Great Glen.

As he passed close to the site where Urquhart Castle now stands, he was drawn to the deathbed of Emchath, an elderly Pictish nobleman. In the raw, precious moments before his passing, Emchath and his family found comfort in the words of the stranger. They spoke of his faith, of death, belief and redemption — and by the light of a fire on the side of Loch Ness, the Christian word was cast.

Inverness Castle

Sandstone and Saltires

The river Ness flows down from the Mighty Glen and swirls beneath the castle walls, dark and strong. The red sandstone crenels and parapets of the battlements stretch across the skyline, and the saltire on the tower flies high over the bustle of life in the Highland capital.

The walls may be young but the soul is old. For a thousand years there has been a fortress here, guarding the way to the mountains and glens. Just as King Donald still walks the banks of the river, so there are ghosts within the walls.

When in 1562, Mary Queen of Scots was refused entry by the castle governor, the clansmen came to the city in their thousands to help the queen — the Munros, the Frasers, the Mackenzies. The castle gates were opened — and the severed head of the governor displayed on the walls as a sign to the wise.

The Heroine and the Prince

Nearly two hundred years later, imagine the red tartans and blue sashes of Bonnie Prince Charlie and his men as they appeared over the hills of Inverness to march on the Hanoverian stronghold. The castle was seized and in one last act of defiant destruction it was razed to the ground. But the Battle of Culloden was waiting in the shadows, poised to inflict a wound so deep that the scar would always remain.

When Bonnie Prince Charlie fled the killing fields of that dark troubled wake, Flora MacDonald risked everything to save the prince. The grounds of the castle celebrate that spirit with her statue — the romance of a dangerous moonlit night and a small boat rowed by a young woman for a prince. The character of a Scottish heroine, forged in granite.

Ballindalloch Castle

The Pearl of the North

Amidst dovecotes, rock gardens and smooth green lawns,
the pearl-grey turrets and ivy-clad walls of Ballindalloch stretch
grandly against a cobalt sky. The sparkling waters of the Avon
and Spey flow swiftly through its moss green meadows,
past grazing cows and fine copper beeches.

Inside, it is the family home of the Macpherson-Grants — a castle
that is rich and alive, warmed by roaring log fires and the glow
of lamps across fine Spanish paintings. From panelled walls
and vaulted halls, the eyes of gilded portraits watch as the
years unfold.

It is a home filled with the spirits of Sea Lords, Majors
and Colonels, all sharing an amber dram of honeyed whisky.
Bide awhile and listen to tales of the high seas, of war and foreign
climes, of stags and grouse and the one that got away.

Drum Castle

A Woodland Jewel

Surrounded by swathes of holly and yew, amidst the ancient oaks of the Old Woods of Drum, the deep rounded walls of the medieval keep have watched over the Irvines of Drum for centuries.

The darkened womb-like walls of the High Hall offered a medieval refuge, where chill winds seeped through tiny windows onto floors of earth and straw. Below it lie the leather bound tomes and glistening rosewood shelves of a Victorian home, where shafts of sunlight fall through long windows onto rich brocade and gilded portraits.

Outside, bowers of copper beech and horse chestnut fall onto manicured lawns, and the walls of a perfect Scottish castle reflect back the glow of the late afternoon sun.

Brodie Castle

Art and Elegance

Amongst the saffron trumpets of sunlit daffodils, the elegant limed walls and corbelled battlements of the castle protect the home of the ancient Brodie clan.

Inside, four centuries of painted ceilings are a backdrop for the rose enamel and glassy white of Chinese porcelain, elegantly placed upon fine French furniture. The panelled walls of high halls and robe rooms are filled with brooding Scottish watercolours and Dutch oils from the Golden Age. Outside an ancient Pictish stone stands guard.

On the night of 20th September 1889, the Earl of Brodie was in Switzerland. That night, the sounds of drawers opening, agitated searching and papers rustling were heard in the study. The butler and servants desperately searched the castle for the study key. It couldn't be found. The noises stopped. In the morning they received the news that the Earl had died suddenly in the night. Maybe he had found what he was looking for that night — he did not need to return.

Kilchurn Castle

This Child of Loud-Throated War

The jagged lines of a time worn stronghold stand at peace now, rising from the glassy depths of Loch Awe, a shadowed footstool to the mighty misted Ben Cruachan.

Tufts of windblown marsh grass and wild hawthorn grow against the ancient rock and stone. The rainbowed fins of salmon shimmer through the fresh clear waters. Here was once the towering fortress of the Clan Campbell and the ancestral home of the Earls of Breadalbane — wild yet stately, desolate yet self-contained amidst the solemn grandeur of the mountains.

Imagine a night when the heavy skies lay low over the darkened hills. Black growls of thunder echoed down the valley and forks of lightning seared across the mountainsides. Kilchurn Castle stood alone, empty but defiant in the teeth of the storm. Suddenly in a moment of blinding light; with the spit and crack of the strike the crown of the castle's tower was hurled deep into the rain lashed earth — where it remains to this day.

The Legend of Kilchurn

Sir Colin Campbell of Glenorchy had been married only a year when he left for the Crusades. He swore to return and gave his young wife, Lady Margaret, one half of his ring as a token of their love. Seven years passed with no news. Neighbouring clans were hungry for power but Margaret kept her faith. One day the dreaded news arrived — Sir Colin had died. The message was a lie, sent by a rival lord.

Unknowingly duped, and desperate to protect the people of her glen, a heartbroken Margaret agreed to marry the traitorous lord. The wedding day arrived and at the castle gates a beggar asked the Lady for some wine. He drank, and handed back the glass — at the base lay her husband's ring. She looked up and into the eyes of Sir Colin. Beneath the disguise, the love she waited for had returned to save his bride.

The Power Within

Kilchurn is silent now; no more loud-throated cries of war, only the whispering of the loch mists around the broken stone walls. The troubled years have passed, when flickering torches led the mighty Campbells to their home, through dark, dank passages underneath the earth. Times when scarlet velvet, silk lace and rich plaids of crimson and green lay beside two handed swords; when tables groaned with silver plates of mutton, beef and fish, and sapphire-studded goblets brimmed with claret and ale.

And all the while, in the cold cavernous depths below the fiery warmth of the hall, there lay the great iron fetters and lengths of heavy chain for prisoners' arms and feet.

Castle Stalker

The Hunter

A prehistoric crannog and an ancient stone keep are glimpsed through a gossamer mist. A blood-red sun sinks in the west and spreads its carmine magic across the outcrops of granite and snow on Creach Bheinn. Calmed now by the gentle lapping of the tides, the brooding parapets and gabled garrets of the tower reflect their thickset shoulders in the depths of Loch Linnhe.

Castle Stalker stands alone, tall and straight, on the rock of cormorants.

The destiny of mighty clansmen, the Stewarts and Campbells, is written in the castle walls — glowering stone that is infused with the dark thunderous red and sombre blackness of revenge. The raging clan fires were stoked by murder and reprisal. The memories of forebears were cherished and a sense of identity burned alive in each generation. The core, the very heart, of a highland conflict was played out on these shores.

Vengeance Burns Brightly

In the shadow of the castle walls to the west there is a small grassy islet. Several hundred years have not changed the view. Imagine the clan chief Alexander Stewart casting his hook and line into the fecund depths of the loch, alone and lost in thought. Unheard, there are stealthy footsteps through the grass. A party of Campbells have seized their chance, and a simmering feud will once again boil over. Fast, deadly and brutal, the sight and sounds of a murder are played out before the castle's eyes.

Hidden deep behind those towering walls, a baby son lost his father to axes and swords. Twenty four years later that son set out to avenge his father's death, crossing the wild glens to Dunstaffnage Castle with the Stewarts of Appin at his side. Nine more men were taken down that night — nine more reasons for revenge.

The hunter once more became the hunted.

To The End

The rugged remains of a castle cling to the cliff, a precipitous drop to the swirling waters of the Moray Firth below.

Moss-covered pillars of stones stand defiantly in the face of the Banffshire wind. A narrow isthmus, flecked with quartz, is surrounded by the relentless pounding of the waves.

When King Haakon of Norway threatened the shores, Findlater was restored — a thirteenth century coastal defence proud and strong.

Abandoned now for four hundred years, the crumbling towers of Findlater were once a mighty home to lowland families; the Ogilvies, Gordons and Sinclairs.

But the sea will return to reclaim its prize. As winter winds and angry waves assault the towering cliffs, ancient walls slowly surrender their fight, and tumble down to the shores below.

So the skeleton of a coastal castle with bones of lichened arches, looks out to sea with hollow eyes in crumbling stones.

Huntly Castle | Mystical Grandeur

The outline of a ruined castle stands amidst the trees where two rivers meet.
A stronghold that once offered shelter to Robert the Bruce; a refuge in the shaded
Aberdeenshire woods.

Heraldic shields and mystical creatures are intricately woven into solid stone walls. They stretch above the door that welcomed those who came to the home of the Gordons of Huntly.

Six hundred years as their spiritual home — the castle grew from simple motte and bailey to a grander palace. The wooden bailey has long since been buried beneath the Renaissance mansion; but the grassy mound of the motte remains — man's indelible changes to the earth made almost nine centuries ago.

Painting the Castles

Colour is an intrinsic part of our lives — it is a raw material in our midst, all around us and forever associated with our actions, feelings and emotions. The brightness and depth of colour seen in Jonathan's paintings are rare in conventional watercolour art and it is this unusual aspect of his work that has become the much loved signature of his growing collection.

When Jonathan first visits a castle he lets the ancient walls start to tell their own story. He will spend hours exploring a castle, viewing it from near and far to develop a sense of the compositions he finds most interesting and exciting. Walk up Salisbury Crags in Edinburgh for example, and you will see the view of Edinburgh Castle that is portrayed on the cover of this

Back in his studio Jonathan uses a mixture of intuition and imagination to select his colours. He chooses them spontaneously as the painting evolves, inspired by the beauty and drama of each castle. The colours may be vivid and intense, but they also feel entirely apt.

Jonathan climbed his first hills when he was five years old and those walks triggered a life long appreciation and passion for mountain scenery. It seems entirely fitting that in Scotland he has found his spiritual home.

This book is a doorway to Scotland's haunting beauty and her rich and passionate heritage. It is an invitation to step further in and explore.

Castles | map

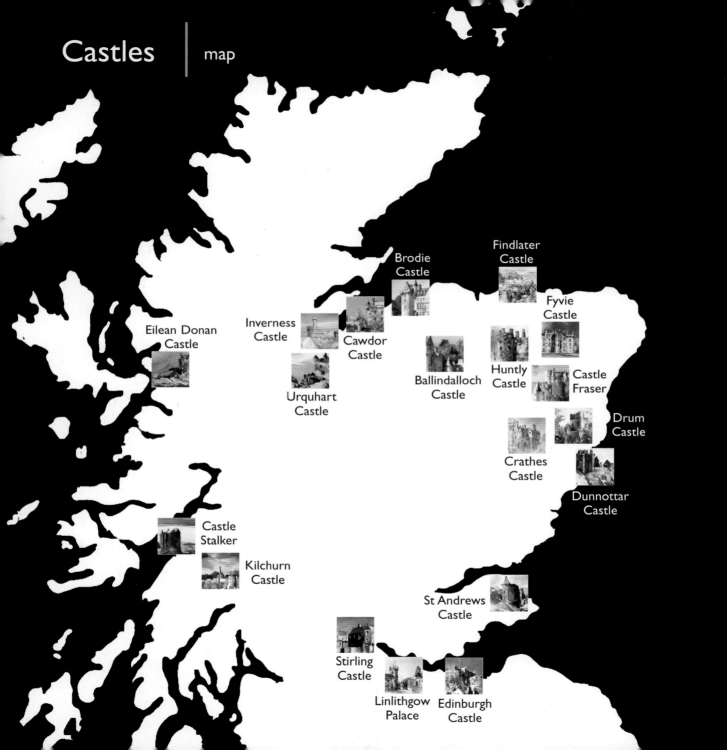

Eilean Donan
Castle

Inverness
Castle

Cawdor
Castle

Brodie
Castle

Findlater
Castle

Fyvie
Castle

Huntly
Castle

Castle
Fraser

Urquhart
Castle

Ballindalloch
Castle

Drum
Castle

Crathes
Castle

Dunnottar
Castle

Castle
Stalker

Kilchurn
Castle

St Andrews
Castle

Stirling
Castle

Linlithgow
Palace

Edinburgh
Castle

Castles | location

 Ballindalloch Castle
On A95, 14 miles north-east of Grantown, AB37 9AX

 Brodie Castle
Off A96, 4.5 miles west of Forres, IV36 2TE

 Castle Fraser
Off B944, 16 miles west of Aberdeen, AB51 7LD

 Castle Stalker
On A828, at Portnacroish, PA38 4BL

 Cawdor Castle
Off B9090, 5.5 miles south-west of Nairn, IV12 5RD

 Crathes Castle
On A93, 3 miles east of Banchory, AB31 5QJ

 Drum Castle
Off A93, 10 miles west of Aberdeen, AB31 5EY

 Dunnottar Castle
On A92, south of Stonehaven, AB39 2TL

 Edinburgh Castle
In the centre of Edinburgh, EH1 2NG

Eilean Donan Castle
On A87, south of Dornie, IV40 8DX

 Findlater Castle
Off A98, 3 miles east of Cullen, AB45 2UD

 Fyvie Castle
Off A947, 8 miles south of Turriff, AB53 8JS

 Huntly Castle
In Huntly off the A96, AB54 4SH

 Inverness Castle
In the centre of Inverness, IV2 3DU

 Kilchurn Castle
On A85, 1 mile west of Dalmally, PA33 1AJ

 Linlithgow Palace
In the centre of Linlithgow, EH49 7AL

 St Andrews Castle
In St Andrews on A91, KY16 9AR

 Stirling Castle
In Stirling, FK8 1EJ

 Urquhart Castle
On A82, at Strone Point, IV63 6XJ

Prints of the castle paintings

Prints of Jonathan's paintings are available for sale at many of the castles featured in this book and at many other good shops around Scotland. All prints are signed by Jonathan individually.

The prints are also available via his website www.jonathanwheelerart.com

Contact Jonathan by email at jonathan@soulofscotland.co.uk